The Good Bonking Guide

Written By:
Herbert Kavet
Illustrated By:
Martin Riskin

Manufactured in the United States of America

30 29 28 27 26 25 24 23 22 21 20 19 18 17 16 15 14 13 12 11 10 9 8 7 6 5 4 3 2 1

Ivory Tower Publishing Co., Inc.
125 Walnut St., Watertown, MA 02172
Telephone #: (617) 923-1111 Fax #: (617) 923-8839

THE MANY DEFINITIONS OF BONKING

Bonking - also screwing, fucking, copulating, boffing, banging, drilling, dipping your wick, scoring, doing it, humping, sexual intercourse, love making, going all the way.

THE ORIGINS OF BONKING

Bonking originally consisted of two lovers literally "bonking" their heads together (usually when they were both reaching to turn out the night light). This was not a fun way to have sex. Over time, people substituted a form of intercourse for the act and the name stuck.

SEASONAL BONKING

There are two schools of thought:

When the weather is hot and sticky
Ain't no time for dunkin' dicky,
But when the frost is on the pumpkin
That's the time for dicky dunkin'.

SEASONAL BONKING

Or:

Hooray Hooray for the first of May
Outdoor bonking begins today.

WHAT MEN THINK THE FIRST TIME THEY BONK

Hey, this is just like jerking off, only you don't have to fantasize.

WHAT WOMEN THINK THE FIRST TIME THEY BONK

Hey, this is just like playing with yourself, only you don't come.

WHY MEN ARE BETTER AT BONKING

Men can come in 43 seconds and then roll over and go right to sleep.

WHY WOMEN ARE BETTER AT BONKING

Women can come 26 times and then want to stay up all night talking about love.

WHAT MEN LIKE BEST ABOUT BONKING

1. Telling their friends.
2. Getting to see lots of naked women.
3. Coming.

WHAT WOMEN LIKE BEST ABOUT BONKING

1. Feeling loved.
2. Coming more than their partner.
3. Seeing their partner droop afterwards.
4. When it's over.

GOOD THINGS TO SAY BEFORE BONKING

Oooh, It's soo big. Please be gentle.
I've had a vasectomy.
Of course I love you.
I've never done this before(women).
Feel my breasts - that's good - harder, harder, slower.

BAD THINGS TO SAY BEFORE BONKING

Isn't that cute.
I've never done this before(men).
Is $50 O.K.?
I thought it would be, well, you know, bigger.

WHAT FOREPLAY MEANS TO WOMEN

Touching

Kissing

Smiling

Caressing

Undressing

Massaging

Sucking

Licking

Sighing

WHAT FOREPLAY MEANS TO MEN

Getting through the list on page 14 as fast as possible.

FAVORITE MALE FOREPLAY TECHNIQUES

1. Unzippng fly while talking about how big it is.
2. Staring at partner's breasts for 20 minutes.
3. Jumping up and down on bed.

FAVORITE MALE FOREPLAY TECHNIQUES

4. Carefully folding underwear to hide the stains.

5. Parading nude in front of mirror while holding stomach in.

6. Advising partner on exercises to reduce and firm her thighs and buttocks.

THINGS MEN SAY DURING FOREPLAY

Why won't you?
Everyone else does it.
You'll get used to it.
I'd do it to you.

THINGS WOMEN SAY DURING FOREPLAY

I hardly know you.
Yes, yes! Feel. Harder, harder, faster.
Scratch my butt, scratch my butt.
A little higher. A little to the left.
Don't touch me there.

5
GREAT FOREPLAY TECHNIQUES

1. Caress your partner's buttocks with the smooth side of a garlic bagel. (For use of the rough side, see the Kinky Sex Chapter.

2. Feed each other Maui Potato chips using only your thighs.

5 GREAT FOREPLAY TECHNIQUES

3 Undress each other using only your teeth.

4. Spread some chocolate Haagen Daz ice cream over your lover's erogenous zones. Slowly lick it off. (Don't let the cleaning lady see the sheets.)

5. Float your partner in a warm bath and use a vibrator on any parts that rise above the surface.

THINGS TO SAY DURING YOUR ORGASM

Aaaaarrragh
Yesyesyesyes
Fuckmefuckmefuckme
Ooooh Aaaah Oouch
ImcomingImcomingImcoming
LarryLarryLarry
(Hopefully your partner's name.)

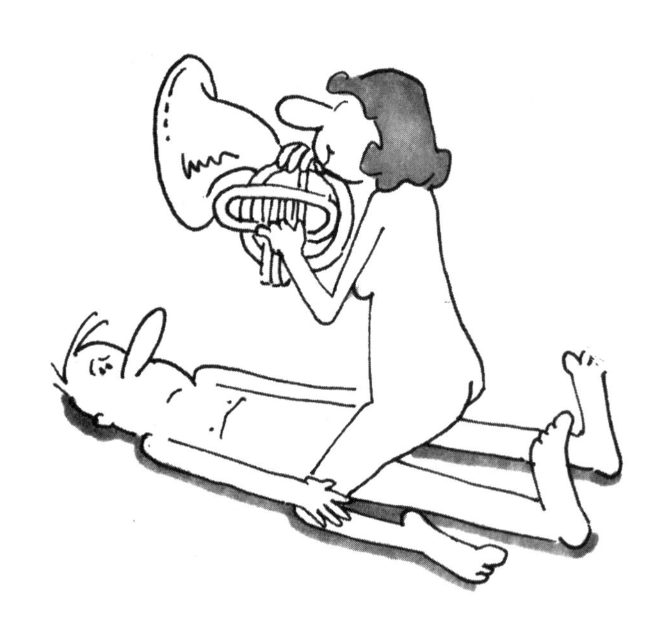

THINGS TO SAY DURING YOUR PARTNER'S ORGASM

Are you done yet?
You're hurting me.
You're really hurting me.
You're doing it wrong.
Do you love me?

WHERE DO FEMALE ORGASMS COME FROM?

- ☐ The vagina
- ☐ The G-Spot
- ☐ The Tooth Fairy
- ☐ A pelvic reaction to screaming obscenities
- ☐ All of the above.
- ☐ No one really knows

No one really knows

WHERE DO MALE ORGASMS COME FROM?

Talking dirty in locker rooms ☐

Exposing a penis to the air ☐
for more than a few seconds

20 seconds of foreplay ☐

An active fantasy life ☐

A tiny feather implanted ☐
beneath the coccyx that wiggles
during copulation

All of the above ☐

All of the above

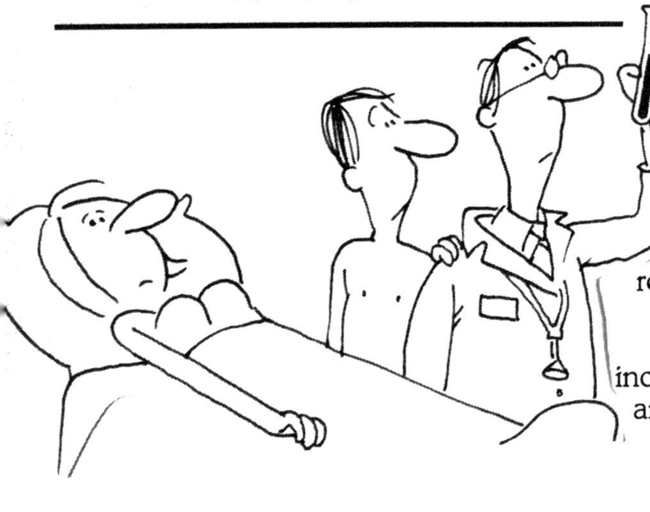

HOW TO TELL IF A PARTNER HAS HAD AN ORGASM

WOMAN

You should realize that there is no way a man can really tell when a woman has had an orgasm. All girls are taught, when still very young, secret acting techniques by their friends and mothers. The techniques include screaming, hysterical laughing, hyperventilation and other noises to confound all but the most perceptive males and a few gynecologists. A hoodwinked male can, however, make a few informed observations.

She may have had an orgasm if:

1. She sleeps soundly and snores like a longshoreman.

2. The lubricating jelly has melted into a puddle.

3. She calls you at work 3 times the following day.

4. She says you can come now.

HOW TO TELL IF A PARTNER HAS HAD AN ORGASM

MAN

Unless you are on a first date, the man, upon orgasm, will immediately roll over and fall soundly asleep. Do not waste your breath talking to him about love, relationships or true happiness.

ADVANTAGES OF BONKING IN THE DARK

1. You can satisfactorily bonk some very ugly people.
2. It's easier to hide cellulite and other embarrassing flab.
3. You're partner may not be able to identify you.
4. It's easy to make faces when engaging in oral sex.
5. It's easy to fake orgasm.

ADVANTAGES OF BONKING IN THE LIGHT

1. You're always sure you have right partner.
2. After a good bonk, you can be sure you'll be properly identified to friends.
3. You can read instruction books to make sure you're doing it right.
4. It's slightly easier to unhook bras.
5. It's much easier to find dropped condoms.

HOW TO BONK ALL NIGHT LONG

WOMEN:

1. Find a great hunk under 19 years of age.
2. Teach him to slow down.
3. Direct him carefully, using simple 2 syllable words like; higher, lower, faster, softer.
4. Stimulate his competitive spirit by keeping a big vibrator on top of your dressing table.

HOW TO BONK ALL NIGHT LONG

MEN:

1. Don't masturbate for a week.
2. Stay away from alcohol.
3. Sprinkle rhino tusk powder on your bran flakes.
4. Tie it to a Q-Tip.

BONKING AND FARTING

It is very impolite to fart while bonking on a first date. What ever will your partner think of you? No, it's better to chance a total explosion of your digestive system than to fart while bonking on a first date.

BONKING AND FARTING

After the first date, it is O.K. to fart while bonking; especially if it is under the covers. People hold the covers down really tight to try to keep the smell in, but this never works. It's especially foolish to do this if your partner's head is under the covers.

CONDOMS

Condoms come in only one size, which means they are either very stretchy or all penises are the same size. Putting on a condom is easy provided the man has an erection. Without an erection, it takes several sets of nimble fingers to hold the thing open and one strong hand to stuff with.

CONDOMS

The only real tough part about using condoms is getting the little foil or plastic packages open. There is no way to do this romantically. Most often the package is opened under the covers using teeth and one hand while trying to continue foreplay with the other.

CIRCUMCISED BONKING

There is no reason why bonking should be any different with a circumcised penis though some women's liberation groups think they are throwing away the best part.

BONKING AND VASECTOMIES

A vasectomy should have no effect on your bonking pleasure if it is performed by a competent surgeon. Don't be like that cheap Jackass who had his vasectomy done at Sears. Every time he gets a hard on, his garage door goes up.

10 GREAT BONKING FANTASIES

1. Tied with leather in the big corral.
2. Cheerleader's shower at Central High.
3. Ice cube tickle with the crotchless panties.
4. Whipped with feathers in the Sultan's Palace.
5. Marooned at sea with 6 Chippendales.

10 GREAT BONKING FANTASIES

6. Spanking naughty co-eds.

7. Ravished by the Gaucho Horde.

8. The vibrating enema.

9. Trading clothes in the hotel elevator.

10. Bath time with the new French Maid.

CALORIES AND BONKING

ACTIVITY	CALORIES BURNED
Getting an erection	
a. On first date	2 calories
If nervous	25 calories
b. With wife	78 calories
c. With someone else's wife	2 calories
When husband shows up	780 calories
d. Failing to get erection	169 calories
e. Failing to get erection for second time	1085 calories

CALORIES AND BONKING

ACTIVITY	CALORIES BURNED
Undressing	
a. Undressing alone	25 calories
b. When partner is laughing at you	225 calories
Removing bra	
a. If a woman	2 calories
b. If a man	53 calories
c. If a man with one hand	275 calories
Removing pantyhose	
a. If a woman	22 calories
b. Partially removing pantyhose	205 calories
c. Forgetting to remove pantyhose	575 calories

CALORIES AND BONKING

ACTIVITY	CALORIES BURNED
Sex Fantasies	
a. Talking partner into fantasy	10 to350 calories depending
b. Laughing at partner's fantasy	25 calories
c. Gathering paraphernalia	162 calories
d. Finding pimple on nose	20 calories
e. Finding pimple "down there"	200 calories
f. Forgetting partner's name	10 calories
g. Hoping partner will forget your name	100 calories

CALORIES AND BONKING

ACTIVITY	CALORIES BURNED
Using the toilet afterwards	
a. Going to the bathroom	50 calories
b. Finding toilet in the dark	75 calories
c. Stepping in kitty litter	162 calories
d. Peeing in closet by mistake(includes clean up)	75 calories
e. Sitting on porcelain when seat was lifted up	120 calories
f. Trying to use toilet quietly	420 calories
g. Making cover-up sounds	125 calories

CALORIES AND BONKING

ACTIVITY	CALORIES BURNED
The morning after	
a. Seeing partner for first time in light	350 calories
b. Finding clothes	25 calories per laugh
c. Not finding clothes	162 calories
d. Acting out fantasy	75 calories
e. Feeling ridiculous	120 calories
f. Convincing partner not to tell friends	420 caloriess

CALORIES AND BONKING

ACTIVITY	CALORIES BURNED
Leaving	
a. Leaving note on pillow	3 calories
b. Long romantic goodbye	50 calories
c. Doing it all over again	250 calories
d. Leaving quickly because husband returned	1050 calories

GOOD THINGS TO SAY DURING BONKING

Ooooh, it's so big.

I've never done this before.

No, my tongue never gets tired.

I could keep this up forever.

After they made you, they threw away the mold.

Ooooh, it's so tight.

Don't stop.

BAD THINGS TO SAY DURING BONKING

What's that smell?

Have you ever done this with a sheep?

The doctor said I should be "clean" by now.

Is the toilet close by?

Is it in?

GOOD THINGS TO SAY AFTER BONKING

You were the best ever.
Yes; 6 times.
It was so big.
We were so together.
Where am I?
You can come now.

BAD THINGS TO SAY AFTER BONKING

Are you finished yet?

What did you say your name is?

I guess you haven't had much experience with this.

Guess what broke.

Don't think you can just go to sleep now.

You did it wrong.

Just leave it on the dresser.

ERECTIONS AND BONKING

It's good to get an erection when:

1. You're alone in an elevator.
2. Dancing real close.
3. Your date touches you.
4. You're bonking. (Erections make bonking much easier.)

ERECTIONS AND BONKING

It's bad to get an erection when:

1. You're in the men's locker room after a round of golf.
2. You're about to zipper your fly.
3. When wearing tight pants and being introduced to date's parents.
4. On a nude beach.

UNDERWEAR FOR BONKING

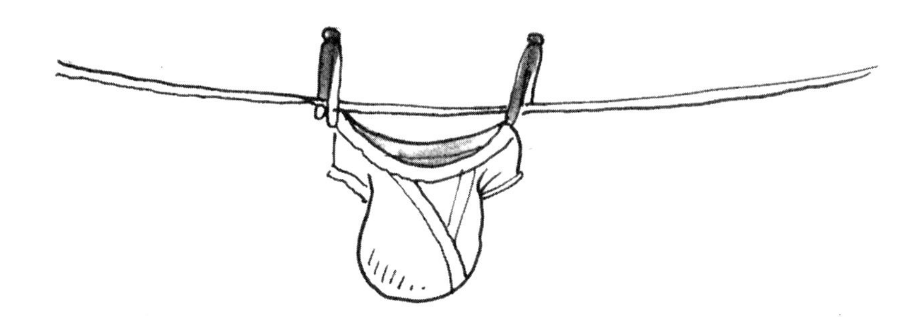

MEN

Boxer Shorts	Very trendy and available in great colors. Always leaves a woman wondering if the guy is trying to hide something.
Briefs	It pays to advertise.
No underwear	Only if you're under 25.

UNDERWEAR FOR BONKING

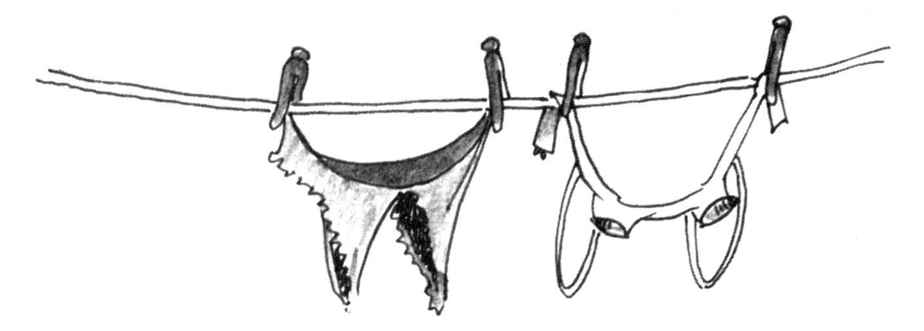

WOMEN

Crotchless	Guys buy these, but no woman has ever worn a pair voluntarily.
Girdles	A great old fashioned deterrent or a turn on for a few misguided perverts such as the artist who's illustrating this book.
French Maid Outfits	The lace and see through is delightful, but who has a figure as good as the models in the catalog?

BONKING ON THE FIRST DATE

Advantages: It's exciting, unexpected, filled with passion and the thrill of the unknown.

There may not be a second date.

BONKING ON THE FIRST DATE

Disadvantages:

You can't imagine how unpleasant a perfectly polite, normal looking stranger can be once the clothes come off.

BONKING WHEN DRUNK

Advantages: Women can be relaxed enough for great orgasms and men numb enough to go on forever.

You have no guilty feelings.

You can bonk people you would never dream of bonking sober.

Disadvantages: You can't remember the good parts.

You can't find your clothes.

When sober, you can't believe the extent to which you've debased yourself.

RECREATIONAL BONKING

Recreational bonking is just for fun and is the sort of bonking men want to do 98% of the time. The other 2% of the time, they try to make babies so their parents will stop bugging them.

ROMANTIC BONKING

Romantic bonking is meaningful, loving and committed bonking and is the sort women prefer to do 98% of the time. The other 2% of the time, women will settle for Recreational Bonking, being a little horny after finally figuring out what to do with Ben Wa balls.

BONKING AND PETS

Curious pets cause more sexual inhibition than the whole Victorian age, flannel nighties and whisker burns put together.

Why Pets Interfere:

1. All pets are curious.

2. Some want to join the fun.

3. Many pets are jealous for the affection.

4. A pet may want to protect its master from what the animal sees as mortal combat.

BONKING AND PETS

You have 4 choices when trying to handle curious pets:

1. Firmness: "Out, Fido, Out!"
2. Substitution: "I'd like to exchange "Mom Cat" for a new girlfriend."
3. Bribing: "See the nice bone."
4. Resignation: "Here, Kitty, hold these panties."

GETTING RID OF A PARTNER AFTER BONKING

Bonking and fun are over, you have to be at the office by 8 and would like to get some sleep. Here are 7 good lines to get rid of a partner.

1. Let's get married.

2. How many men have you slept with?

3. On a scale of 10, I'd give tonight a definite 9. That restaurant you took me to was 8 alone.

4. Guess where Ernie and the guys on the video crew are hidden.

GETTING RID OF A PARTNER AFTER BONKING

5. The reason I'm jittery is that Rocko usually comes by around now. He and his stupid knives.

6. I've been itchy like this all week. Every hair seems to be on fire.

7. Do you always smell like that after sex?

TIME SPENT ON BONKING

Middle-aged Married People	Spend equal time finding a partner, finding a place away from home to do it, actually bonking and ultimately getting rid of the partner before the husband or wife finds out.
Old Folks	Don't have to spend much time finding an older partner or place to do it, but the bonking itself takes lots of time. It now takes them all night to do what they used to do all night. Getting rid of partners takes no time since after bonking, they usually can't stand one another.

TIME SPENT ON BONKING

Teenagers	70% of their time is spent trying to find a partner and 25% of their time is spent trying to find a place to do it. They spend only 5% of their time actually bonking and they never try to get rid of a willing partner.
Young Adults	Divide their time equally between finding a bonking partner, bonking and getting rid of the partner.

KINKY BONKING

Kinky sex will add another dimension to your bonking pleasure. Unimaginable pleasures emerge from playing all the games you have ever fantasized about. You have to, of course, talk your partner into these little idiosyncrasies.

TALKING YOUR PARTNER INTO KINKY SEX

1. Talk about it realistically, maturely and with dignity.
2. Calm his or her shrieking or hysterical laughter while you explain why the rubber sheets, zucchini, goldfish and Japanese swing are really necessary for your total fulfillment.
3. Resign yourself to having all your partner's friends refer to you as that wierdo, from now on.

KINKY BONKING GOING TOO FAR

It's easy to get carried away with kinky fantasies. You've gone too far when:

1. Your partner faints.
2. Your partner gags.
3. Your partner slides off the apparatus and into the next apartment.
4. The neighbors complain about the goat droppings.

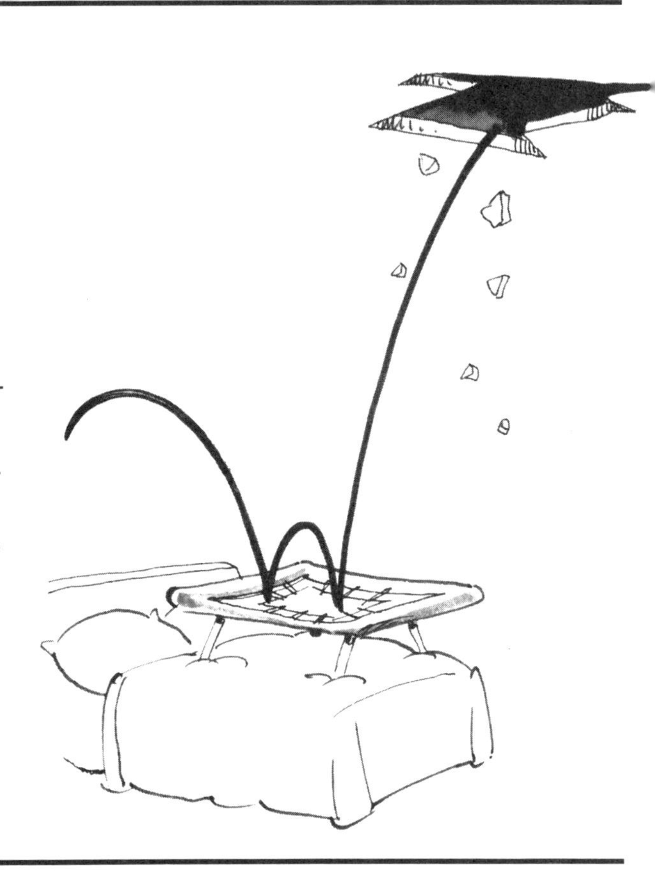

KINKY BONKING GOING TOO FAR

5. Your partner physically attacks you(unless that is part of your fantasy).

6. The water starts to leak into the kids' room.

7. A tongue gets so swollen that intelligible speech is no longer possible.

KINKY BONKING CALMING A HORRIFIED PARTNER

First, calmly put away the oils, the enemas, the chains and leather, the vibrators and the chicken suits. Then decide which of the 3 guaranteed methods of calming a horrified partner you will use.

KINKY BONKING CALMING A HORRIFIED PARTNER

The three methods:

1. Forget it. "O.K., we tried it and you didn't like it. We'll forget it."

2. Modify it. "How about we'll use a smaller vibrator and less ice in the peanut oil."

3. Repeat it. "We'll just give it another chance. I'm sure you'll get used to it."

WHEN TO BONK

Not everyone bonks just prior to going to bed in the evening. Some perfectly normal perverts find other times during the day.

Mornings	Weirdos, artists, punkos, non-working people, horny insomniacs. Honeymooners.
Afternoons	Husbands & wives with other people's husbands & wives. Honeymooners.

WHEN TO BONK

Evenings	Single people, lovers, romantics. Honeymooners.
Before Bedtime	Normal people who work the next day. Honeymooners.
Christmas & Fourth of July	Parents of young children.

BONKING AFTER MARRIAGE

Bonking after marriage is different than when you were single. When you were single, you took time for romance and foreplay and multiple orgasm and everything. After marriage, it seems enough to take care of the business at hand, roll over and go to sleep trying to avoid the wet spot.

BONKING AFTER MARRIAGE

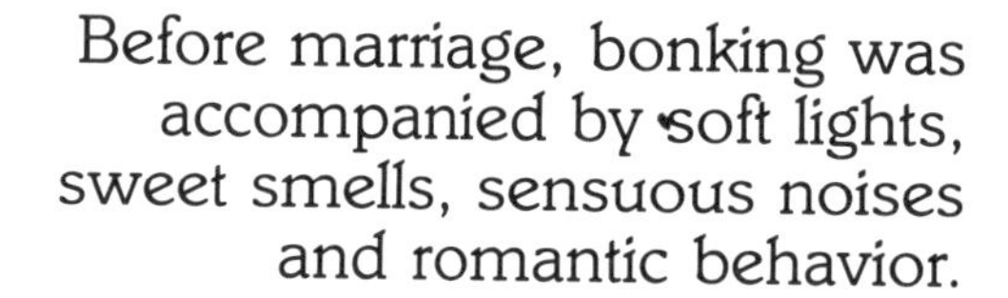

Before marriage, bonking was accompanied by soft lights, sweet smells, sensuous noises and romantic behavior.

After marriage, bonking is accompanied by money fights, headaches, babies, sexy VCR movies and incredibly skimpy(for your current weight) lacy underclothes.

BONKING AFTER CHILDREN

The Ten Commandments

I. Thou shalt not expect privacy when retiring to the bedroom.

II. Thou shalt not keep sex paraphernalia, no matter how well hidden, because the kids will find it.

III. Thou shalt not rent sexy videos because the kids will watch them.

IV. Thou shalt not lock the bedroom door because the kids will listen at the crack.

V. Thou shalt not expect peace when on vacation because the baby sitter will call.

BONKING AFTER CHILDREN

The Ten Commandments

VI. Thou shalt not expect thy lingerie drawer to remain secret from your children's friends.

VII. Thou shalt not keep condoms because they will be blown up as balloons.

VIII. Thou shalt not keep sex books because they will be taken to show and tell.

IX. Thou shalt not make noises of pleasure because they will wake infants.

X. Thou shalt be especially careful making more little brothers and sisters.

ADVANCED BONKING
THE SIMULTANEOUS ORGASM

Simultaneous orgasms are a wonderful goal to work towards while you're bonking. Sort of like a final exam. A few couples find them easy to achieve, but most find the deft sense of timing, the endurance and the delicate balance elusive.

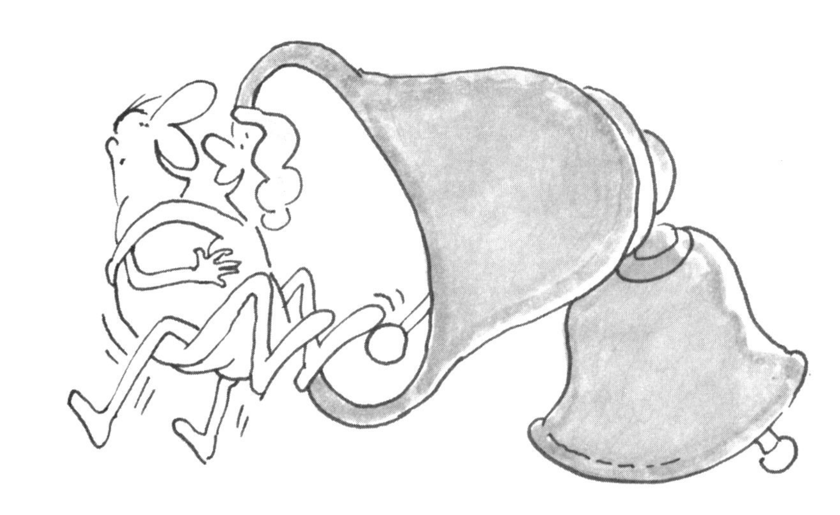

ADVANCED BONKING

THE SIMULTANEOUS ORGASM

Watch out for people who claim to have simultaneous orgasm all the time. They probably lie about other things as well.

Most people think simultaneous orgasms are not an objective, but more of a miracle.

BONKING PROBLEMS

FAILURE TO ACHIEVE ORGASM

The most common reasons for failure to achieve orgasm are:

1. Not in the mood.

2. Incompetent foreplay.

3. Married to person you're in bed with.

4. Not married to person you're in bed with.

FAILURE TO ACHIEVE ORGASM

5. Partner not really trying.

6. Partner has moustache and you are a man.

7. Partner wears bra and you are a woman.

BONKING PROBLEMS

FRIGIDITY

The 6 main causes of frigidity in women are:

1. Partner asks how long you are going to take.
2. Partner calls you by wrong name.
3. You think you hear kids or parents at door.

FRIGIDITY

4. Partner confesses to being gay.

5. You're afraid of someone coming into the room, especially your husband.

6. Partner's religious medallion keeps bashing you in the nose.

OTHER BONKING PROBLEMS

Baldness	Caused by over excited partner pulling out hair.
Bad Teeth	Usually caused by excessive practice of oral sex.

OTHER BONKING PROBLEMS

Loss of Memory	Bonking is frequently associated with poor memory, for example, forgetting whether or not one is married.
Zipped Penis	Caused by rushing to get into trousers when large husband or lover returns early.

EXCUSES FOR NOT BONKING

Even the most ardent bonker occassionally needs a night off. Here are 10 good excuses that should get you a good nights sleep without offending your partner.

1. I'm sore (weak if you haven't bonked for a month).

2. The kids are listening (helpful to have kids).

3. My mother is listening.

4. My mother is not listening (for kinky lover).

5. I have such a headache the sound of an erection would split my brain.

EXCUSES FOR NOT BONKING

6. I can get it up alright, I'm just tired.

7. Again? We just did it last month.

8. It's the bladder infection.

9. It's that time of the month again? Again?

10. I hardly know you (awkward if married).

BONKING ALL NIGHT LONG

Only two types of lovers can bonk all night long:

1. People under 23 years old.

2. People showing off for partners under 23 and you'd better believe they'll pay for it the next day.

BONKING ALL NIGHT LONG

Advantages: The stuff of legends. Great for your reputation and great to tell friends about.

Disadvantages: You'll probably be so sore it'll hurt to pee for 3 days.

BONKING WITH FOREIGNERS

Foreigners make exciting and exotic bonking partners. Bonking these people is the same as bonking regular folks except they have hard-to-pronounce names and they may have unusual and interesting sex customs and diseases. Always see your doctor after bonking foreigners.

BONKING WITH FOREIGNERS

Bonking foreigners can introduce you to some very whimsical sex practices. Some people, of course, may find bonking with a 16" Kabobo club up their you know what while 3 witch doctors dance around your mat a little too capricious.

RATING YOUR BONKING

A Good Bonker

A good bonker doesn't ask how you are doing; does kiss you before falling asleep; volunteers to sleep on the wet spot and is not disturbed by loud farting.

RATING YOUR BONKING

A Bad Bonker

A bad bonker has cold hands and feet; keeps TV on so as not to waste time; knows only 2 positions and moves only to go to the bathroom.

10 COMMANDMENTS OF BONKING

I. Thou shalt not skimp on foreplay.

II. Thou shalt indulge your partner's fantasies no matter how idiotic.

III. Thou shalt not climax before your partner.

IV. Thou shalt engage in at least a little afterplay before falling asleep.

V. Thou shalt encourage your partner to reach multiple orgasms especially on weekends.

VI. Thou shalt not not make fun of your partner's insufficiencies.

VII. Thou shalt not make faces during oral sex.

VIII. Thou shalt endure excruciatingly uncomfortable positions if they really make your partner happy.

IX. Thou shalt search diligently for erogenous zones.

X. Thou shalt not speak about your bonking experiences with anyone but your best friend.